Original title:
Let's Hibernate Already

Copyright © 2024 Creative Arts Management OÜ
All rights reserved.

Author: Rafael Sterling
ISBN HARDBACK: 978-9916-94-252-9
ISBN PAPERBACK: 978-9916-94-253-6

Snow-laden Silhouettes

As the frost begins to creep,
I dream of snoozing, oh so deep.
Blankets piled, a cozy mound,
In fluffy clouds, I'm tightly bound.

Chill winds whisper, 'Take a break!'
While hot cocoa's sweet embrace I take.
The snowflakes twirl, a dance so spry,
Yet here I am, just passing by.

Socks mismatched, a playful sight,
In this lazy, wintry night.
The world outside a snowy blast,
But in my dreams, I'm having a blast.

So let the winds swirl, the snowflakes twine,
I'll keep this napping, it feels just fine.
With every snooze, a giggle escapes,
In my cozy cave, it's joy my heart tapes.

The Serenity of Snowbound Spaces

In cozy nooks we burrow down,
Hot cocoa sipping, no need to frown.
The world outside is white and still,
Inside, we're wrapped in blankets, chill.

The snowflakes dance, they swirl and glide,
While we just laugh and stay inside.
Why face the cold, the sleet, the rain?
Let's bask in warmth, ignore the pain.

When Nature Takes a Breath

The trees are bare, the branches sigh,
Underneath, the critters lie.
They dream of spring, but here we are,
Cozy as a cat, no need for a car.

The world slows down, a quiet thrill,
As frosty winds give us a chill.
We chuckle softly, in our nests,
Winter's coddled, in the best of quests.

Silence Settles Softly

The hush of snow, it fills the air,
We're wrapped up snug, without a care.
No need to rush, no friendly fight,
We'll snooze till morning, out of sight.

The world can wait, it's frozen still,
With everything resting, it's a thrill.
Under our blankets, we find peace,
Winter's quiet grants us sweet release.

Winter's Repose

The world's an ice rink, slick and bright,
Yet here we lounge, all snug and tight.
Not a single urgent task in sight,
Just crispy snacks and dimmed moonlight.

We'll save the world for warmer days,
For now, let's nap in cozy ways.
In winter's hold, we find our bliss,
With all this rest, who'd want to miss?

Resting with the Earth

In cozy burrows, snug and tight,
A blanket of leaves feels just right.
Animal friends, all snoozing sound,
While dreams of snacks dance all around.

Winter's chill calls us to retreat,
To snuggle deep in our comfy seat.
With cocoa dreams and soft pillows,
We drift away like sleeping meadows.

Under the Veil of the Snow

Beneath the flakes, the ground is still,
Worms and bugs are quiet at will.
Nature's pause, a giggly spree,
We're all wrapped up like a big burrito, you see.

Fluffy snowflakes are falling down,
Covering us like a winter gown.
While squirrels chuckle in their laid-back lair,
It's time for bed, without a care!

The Long Sleep of December

December whispers soft and low,
Time for slumber, let it flow.
The world outside is icy and bright,
We snore and dream throughout the night.

With hot cocoa and cuddly bears,
We brave the cold, without any cares.
As stars twinkle above the night,
Our snoozing souls are quite the sight.

A Pause in Time

Tick-tock goes the winter clock,
But outside, nature takes a dock.
Grass is sleeping, trees are still,
Taking a break, and what a thrill!

In the quiet, laughter grows,
As naps unfold, and snuggles flow.
With warm thoughts and fuzzy delight,
Let's call it quits, and say goodnight!

Hibernation's Gentle Call

The sun is dim, the chill is near,
A blanket's warmth is what I cheer.
The couch is calling, oh so sweet,
With snacks and dreams, it can't be beat.

The world outside is cold and gray,
But here I'll nap the winter away.
The snowflakes dance, but I won't budge,
As soft as toast, I'm snug as a grudge.

Beneath the Icicle Veil

Icicles hanging from the eaves,
While under quilts, I plot and weave.
With cocoa sips and popcorn puffs,
I hug my pillow, winter's tough!

The frosty air, it bites and stings,
But I'm a bear with snuggy things.
So let it snow, let tempests roar,
I've got my snacks, I need no more.

Winter's Lullaby

The wind it howls, the nights are long,
In cozy corners, I belong.
A cozy nook, a book in hand,
The frosty world, I'll just withstand.

A warm embrace from fluff and fleece,
The world outside sits in a freeze.
The winter tunes, soft on repeat,
My eyes grow heavy, off to sleep!

Napping Under a Frosty Moon

The stars are bright, but I won't go,
I'd rather snooze and steal the show.
The moon above, a silver light,
Says, 'Stay inside, it's not polite.'

A leap and flop, I take my place,
In summer dreams, I quicken pace.
While snowflakes dance in crisp night air,
I'll keep my dreams in winter's lair.

The Peace of the Unseen

In shadows deep, the sofa waits,
The remote is lost, food on plates.
Pajamas cheer, they rule the day,
With snacks surrounding, we laugh and play.

Blankets piled, a fortress's might,
Tucked in cozy, it's pure delight.
We slip and slide through dreams so sweet,
While life outside just skips a beat.

Frosty Fables and Calming Tales

Snowflakes dance in a dreamlike waltz,
While we sip cocoa, no faults at all.
The world may freeze, but here it's warm,
Wrapped in tales and a comfy charm.

Curled in corners, the cat snores loud,
Even dog takes naps, so nonchalant, proud.
We chase the clouds through the afternoon,
With chuckles echoing, like a sweet tune.

In the Heart of the Storm

Thunder drums as the winds do howl,
Yet here we hide, no need to scowl.
The weather's wild, a circus act,
While snacks flow freely, that's a fact.

Fluffy slippers are our brave shoes,
Climbing to comfort, we never lose.
Through storms we giggle, a jolly crew,
With each gust outside, we laugh anew.

A Pause in the World's Rhythm

The clock ticks slow, a gentle tease,
Time stands still, just as we please.
Outside there's chaos, but here it's calm,
With ticklish laughter and warm palm.

The fridge hums loudly, a friendly tune,
As we raid it once more like raccoons in June.
With every bite, giggles arise,
In this cozy space, we're experts in sighs.

Moments Wrapped in Warmth

Blankets piled high,
Cocoa in a cup,
As the chill winds sigh,
Together we warm up.

Sweaters, socks, and hats,
The fashionista's flair,
Lost amidst the chats,
We're cozy without care.

Fuzzy slippers glide,
Across the chilly floor,
Cuddles can't subside,
Who could ask for more?

In this snug retreat,
Time slowly drifts by,
With laughter so sweet,
We'll wave the cold goodbye.

Beneath the Hearth's Glow

Crackling firelight,
Dances in the dark,
Snuggled up so tight,
It's quite the lark.

Popping corn and cheer,
As shadows start to play,
We've nothing to fear,
Just whimsies on display.

Stoking up the vibe,
With stories spun from dreams,
Laughter we prescribe,
As our hearts burst at the seams.

This is where we thrive,
In warmth and silly glee,
While the cold arrives,
We toast to harmony.

Chasing the Last Leaves

Crunching leaves abound,
As autumn bids goodbye,
We giggle, twirl around,
  With a hint of a sigh.

Sweaters growing tight,
From feasts of turkey pie,
'Twas a glorious night,
As the branches fly high.

Dancing in the air,
With pumpkin-spiced delight,
We chase without a care,
  Until it's out of sight.

Yet here comes the coo,
Of the chilly breezes tall,
Come join the hullabaloo,
As winter starts to call.

The Welcome of the Long Nights

Evenings stretch so wide,
As daylight starts to fade,
With snacks upon our side,
Our plans are cleverly laid.

Netflix close at hand,
And popcorn in a bowl,
A couch so well planned,
Is the perfect role.

Jokes shared by the fire,
And laughter fills the air,
In warmth we conspire,
To forget winter's stare.

So grab your warmest gear,
Let the long nights unfurl,
With giggles, don't you fear,
We'll dance in our own whirl.

Tranquility Amongst the Trees

In the woods where squirrels dream,
The leaves are plotting, or so it seems.
Trees wear blankets made of snow,
Whispering secrets they only know.

Bears yawn wide, stretching with grace,
While rabbits find their cozy place.
The winter sun, a lazy friend,
Brings warmth before the day's end.

The Still Sanctuary

Icicles dangle, a crystal show,
Bears grab pajamas, snug as a bow.
Rabbits play cards with a deer and a fox,
While sleepy owls count the ticking clocks.

Fireside tales of warm, sunny days,
Frosty air with a nutty haze.
Polar bears dream of beaches and sand,
Hoping for summer's gentle hand.

A Tapestry of Frost

Snowflakes dance in a chilly ballet,
Foxes wear scarves in a quirky way.
The snowman grins, a toothy delight,
As penguins slide through the silvery white.

Bunnies build fortresses, soft and grand,
Sipping hot cocoa pooled in their hand.
Frosty mornings, a whimsical sight,
With critters breaking into laughter so bright.

The Peace in the Plummet

Down the hill, the sleds take flight,
Racers zoom past, shouts of delight.
The snow is powder, the chill is grand,
While chipmunks are busy plotting their stand.

With every tumble, laughter erupts,
In winter's grasp, everyone disrupts.
Snowmen wobble, but stand so proud,
Creating coziness in a frosty crowd.

In the Cradle of Cold

Snowflakes dance, oh what a show,
My fuzzy socks are all aglow.
The couch is calling, it's time to rest,
With cookies and cocoa, I'm feeling blessed.

Blankets piled, a mountain high,
Outside the window, the chilly sigh.
The fridge is stocked, I've got my game,
To hibernate here, oh please, no shame!

Where Time Slows Down

The clock ticks slow, it's quite absurd,
As I lounge around, feeling like a bird.
With binging shows and snacks galore,
No need to rush, who wants to score?

Pajama days are all the rage,
Each meal a feast, I'm on this stage.
Why lift a finger when I can stare,
At the wonders of my cozy lair?

Wrapped in Winter's Embrace

The chill outside is here to stay,
Inside my fort, I gladly lay.
With popcorn bowls and laughter near,
I'm king of comfy - give a cheer!

The world can freeze, let it snow or sleet,
I own this blanket, I claim the seat.
With every sip of herbal tea,
I'm the warmest, happiest me!

The Stillness Between Seasons

The squirrels are snoozing, what a sight,
While I'm here dreaming, oh so right.
The fire crackles, it's all so nice,
Might just stay here, think twice, think thrice.

My plants are resting, they don't complain,
It's the perfect pause before spring's reign.
With cozy socks and a lazy flair,
I declare it's bliss in my snowy lair!

Emblems of Eternal Rest

Beneath a blanket, snug and tight,
I'll snooze away the frosty night.
With snacks and tea, I'll hibernate,
While snowflakes dance and squirrels wait.

A fuzzy sock on every foot,
My cozy chair is where I'm put.
The world outside can freeze and freeze,
I'll trade the chill for cozy ease.

The sun can call, but I won't budge,
The couch, my throne, I'll never judge.
As bears do in their cave of dreams,
I'll drift away on comfy beams.

When spring arrives, I'll hear it clear,
But for now, let the ice appear.
I'll snooze and snore 'til flowers sprout,
In fuzzy joy, I have no doubt.

A Nest of Tranquility

In layers thick, I take my stand,
A quiet nook, my favorite land.
The world can shout, but I won't shout,
In blissful peace is what it's about.

With popcorn, pillows, all around,
No need to seek where fun is found.
While winter winds whip quickly past,
My cozy nest ensures I last.

The chill may nip, it may insist,
But I've a blanket, I'm not missed.
A midnight snack, a snooze or two,
In hibernation, dreams come true.

So let it snow, let cold winds wail,
I'll ride my dreams on frosty trails.
Why brave the world with all its fuss?
I'll snooze away, what's wrong with us?

The Heartbeat of Winter

With each soft thud, my heart does hum,
In sleepy realms, I've found my drum.
The world outside may start to freeze,
   I'd rather take a nap with ease.

A heated cup, a fuzzy hat,
I'll tuck away on my plush mat.
While others rush with winter gear,
I'll huddle close without a fear.

Let little critters dart and play,
While I just dream the hours away.
With snowflakes falling, I retreat,
To joyfully doze and softly beat.

So call my name, I won't respond,
My peaceful realm is quite the bond.
In winter's arms, I'm lost, that's true,
This sleepy hibernation's due.

Snowdrift Dreams

In drifts of white, I curl and grin,
The world can wait; I'm tucked within.
With warmest dreams and snuggly gears,
I'll laugh and snooze through all my fears.

As flakes cascade like gentle sighs,
I'll input cozy, no need for ties.
The outside chaos can't intrude,
I'll nap away, in solitude.

Oh, drifts of snow, so pure and bright,
They urge me not to fight the night.
I'll keep my dreams both soft and light,
And laugh with joy at winter's bite.

So let them call, I'll pull my shade,
In snowdrift dreams my heart is laid.
With cozy moments, I shall claim,
The gift of rest, my winter fame.

The Yearning for Stillness

As the world slows its pace,
With coffee cups held tight,
There's a call to the blankets,
To embrace the couch tonight.

The chill in the air sings,
A symphony of cold feet,
Our favorite show awaits,
So cozy down, take a seat.

The cat claims the warm spot,
While we laugh at the snow,
Staying put feels just right,
Why venture out? No, no!

Fuzzy socks and hot soup,
A snow day, pure delight,
Dreaming of hibernation,
As we snuggle in tight.

In the Embrace of Long Nights.

The sun takes its long break,
While the moon starts to glow,
Time for snacks and reruns,
In our lair of warm flow.

Fluffy blankets entice,
To stay snug, just for fun,
The cold can keep its chill,
While we huddle as one.

Outside, the dogs leap,
In their coats made of fluff,
But we're happy inside,
Where the weather's not tough.

A kingdom of cozy,
With cocoa in hand,
We'll swirl in our cushions,
In our winter wonderland.

Winter's Gentle Embrace

A blanket wrapped so tight,
Like a hug from the frost,
The fireplace is crackling,
Comfy warmth at no cost.

Snowflakes dance outside,
But who cares, let them fall?
We'll start our own blizzard,
With popcorn, snacks, and all.

The world may be frosty,
But inside, it feels right,
Staying put in our fortress,
Through the long, cozy night.

So pull the curtains closed,
And surrender to cheer,
Winter's gentle embrace,
Keeps our laughter near.

Slumber in Snowflakes

The snow piles up high,
While we dive into dreams,
The world outside shivers,
We're wrapped up in our schemes.

Let the wind howl its tune,
As we nap on the couch,
Instead of turning out,
We'll just stay like a slouch.

The cold can do its best,
We've got snacks by our side,
With a warm mug in hand,
Let this snow day be wide.

While winter plays its game,
We'll find joy in this space,
A slumber of snowflakes,
In our cozy embrace.

When Daylight Retreats

As daylight fades and shadows creep,
I'm ready for my cozy heap.
The world's a chill, oh what a tease,
Let's snuggle up, oh yes please!

With snacks stacked high beside my bed,
I'll whisper secrets to my head.
The couch has called, I can't resist,
A nap awaits, that's my to-do list!

The sun can shine, it's just not fair,
I'd rather snooze without a care.
The world can wait, I've hit my snooze,
Just let me wear my comfy shoes!

When winter's chill wraps all in white,
I'll dream of warmth while tucked in tight.
A blissful state, so soft and sweet,
Let's celebrate this lazy feat!

Embracing the Quiet

In the hush of snow, time slows down,
I sport my favorite yawn and frown.
The world can twirl and spin away,
I'll cozy up and dream all day.

The squirrels jump high, but I stay low,
Beneath the blankets, I'll never go.
While others freeze with coats so neat,
I'm in my PJs, can't be beat!

It's a slumber party of one plus me,
Embracing quiet, pure jubilee.
Let the frosty winds howl and blow,
I'm tucked away, don't need the show.

With every sip of cocoa warm,
I'll ride out winter's snowy storm.
The world moves on, but I'm just fine,
In my cozy fort, I'll sip my wine!

The Deep Slumber Awakens

When the sun dips low and shadows yawn,
I find my place, the day is gone.
A mound of pillows is my throne,
Next to the snacks I call my own.

The night creeps in, with dreams aglow,
I'm off to lands where good snacks grow.
While others frolic, I take my cue,
With wild snoring, and maybe a chew!

Oh, the pleasure of dozing so deep,
With sweet adventures, not a peep.
Encased in warmth, a sleepy delight,
Tomorrow can wait till the sunlight's bright.

With cozy blankets wrapped tight,
My eyes close softly, fading from sight.
In slumber's grip, my dreams take flight,
A joyful heart in the still of the night!

Frosty Naps and Dreaming Days

Frosty air and a wind that bites,
Makes me want to lock up tight.
With fluffy socks and a steaming mug,
I'll find my cave, just a little snug.

The world outside is frosted slow,
While I'm inside, it's nap-time's show.
Let snowflakes dance and swirl around,
I'll be dreaming 'til spring's profound.

With a blanket fortress wrapped around,
I'll dive into dreams, so blissfully bound.
The sun may shine, but let it be,
I'm in my happy realm, just me and my tea.

So here's to winter, short and sweet,
In the warmth of dreams, I'm never beat.
Frosty naps and dreaming days,
Bring on the slumber, in fluffy ways!

The Safety of Softness

Fluffy blankets hug me tight,
Cuddle up, it feels just right.
Pajamas warm, a cozy spree,
Who needs the world? Just you and me.

The couch becomes my favorite throne,
In this kingdom, I'm alone.
Snack stash piled up to the brim,
In this realm, my chances are slim.

Furry friends, they snore with glee,
Their dreams of chasing squirrels, you see.
I join the nap, a perfect blend,
Softness and sleep, my ultimate friend.

Refuge from the Ravaging Storm

The wind outside is quite a show,
Like a toddler with too much glow.
Rain dances mad upon the street,
In here, we're safe, oh so sweet!

Tea brewed strong, the kettle sings,
While wild winds throw their flings.
Is that thunder? No, it's my cat,
She's plotting world domination, imagine that!

The shutters rattle, but we play on,
With every storm, my couch is dawn.
Board games stacked, we make our stand,
In this haven, it's simply grand!

Time Slows in the Snow

The snowflakes fall, a slow ballet,
Outside's a wonderland of play.
But here inside, oh what a treat,
No boots or coats, just socks on my feet.

Tick-tock goes the clock with flair,
Minutes stretch; I really don't care.
Hot cocoa swirling, marshmallows afloat,
Time slows down on this comfy boat.

A montage of cuddles, blankets galore,
Adventure? Not today, I implore!
With each flake, my plans disappear,
Snow may swirl, but quiet is near.

Cocoons of Comfort

Wrapped up tight in my fluffy nest,
This cocoon of comfort is simply the best.
I peek out once, but the world looks cold,
I'll stay right here, doth I not feel bold?

Fuzzy thoughts come in a parade,
Plotting naps with grand charades.
Fictional lands overrun with cheese,
In dreams, maybe I'll travel with ease.

So here I'll lie, the world's a bore,
In soft little layers, I'll snore some more.
With a cozy hum and a satisfied grin,
In these arms of comfort, I'll just stay in.

A Time to Drift in Dreams

Cozy blankets piled up high,
A warm cocoon where I can lie.
The world outside is gray and bleak,
But in here, it's the dreamer's peak.

Pajamas snug, a fluffy throne,
I reign here and I'm not alone.
With snacks and shows, I plan my reign,
Hibernation, oh sweet refrain!

The cold winds howl, but I don't care,
My fortress built beyond compare.
Bring on the snooze, the soft embrace,
Winter's grip, I face with grace.

So let them shiver, I'll just grin,
In this cozy, cheerful din.
While snowflakes dance beneath the sun,
I'll snooze away—oh what a fun run!

Slipping Away from the Cold

As winter wraps its icy arms,
I drift away from all its charms.
The chill outside can have its fun,
While I slip into the warmth, well-done.

The fire crackles, popcorn pops,
I shuffle 'round in fuzzy flops.
Hot cocoa served, the marshmallows float,
With each sip, my worries smote.

Snow may blanket the world with white,
But I find joy in the soft twilight.
Let frostbite tease with brisk embrace,
I'll cuddle tighter in my space.

So let it snow, let winds blow wild,
I'm not bothered, I'm winter's child.
With comfy socks and a happy sigh,
I blend with blankets, oh me, oh my!

Embracing the Season of Stillness

The world is quiet, winter's tune,
Under a blanket, I'll croon.
Snowflakes swirl like a soft ballet,
While I revel in this grand delay.

With a pot of stew and a lazy cat,
I've mastered the art of the cozy spat.
Outside's a howling icy beast,
In here's a feast—let's cuddle and feast!

The frost may pinch with fingers sharp,
But I find solace in this harp.
Strumming dreams by the fireside glow,
The season of stillness is my show.

So let the world in winter stand,
I'll be right here, a hot mug in hand.
With giggles bubbling in my core,
Here's to stillness—who could want more?

Gentle Surrender to Slumber

When outside's a frozen fairyland,
I wrap myself in dreams so grand.
Soft flannel sheets and a pillow hug,
   I'm here to drift, snug as a bug.

The wind may whistle, the frost may bite,
But in my cocoon, it's pure delight.
As shadows creep and daylight wanes,
I surrender now, my mind unchains.

While snowmen bobble with goofy grins,
I'll snooze 'til dawn, where warmth begins.
With sleepy giggles and eyelids droop,
I float to dreams, a slumber swoop.

So let the chill chase everyone near,
I'll hibernate without any fear.
In this gentle lull, I cast away,
Tomorrow's worries until they decay!

Surrender to the Stillness

In the depths of winter's grasp,
I find myself in cozy clasp.
Socks are fuzzy, blankets tight,
Time to nap, oh what a sight!

The fridge is packed with snacky treats,
Sitting here, no need for feats.
While the world wears icy coats,
I'm just a bear, without the oats.

A distant howl, a frosty breeze,
I raise my mug, prepare to please.
Hot cocoa flows like rivers warm,
Against the cold, I'll ride the storm!

So, fellow friends, come join the cheer,
Let's curl up and disappear.
For winter's chill can wait outside,
While we snuggle with warm pride.

The Breath of Frost-filled Air

With every breath, the chill does bite,
I bundle up, it feels just right.
The outside world a frosted dream,
Here I am, a cozy seam.

A penguin waddle to the door,
One step out, and I want more!
Back to warmth, I must retreat,
This couch is where I claim my seat.

Oh, winter air, you tempt me so,
But I would rather not be cold, you know.
Wrapped in layers, oh so plush,
I'll greet the snow with a slow hush.

So let the iceflakes dance and twirl,
While I savor my coffee swirl.
A world of frost, a world of fun,
But my hibernation's just begun.

Seeking Warmth in the Quiet

Quiet hours, the snowflakes fall,
I'm tucked away, enjoying it all.
The world outside can stay so white,
    All's calm in my cozy site.

Candles flicker, shadows dance,
In this warmth, I find my chance.
    Fluffy slippers on my toes,
    I'm basically a sleepy rose.

Blankets piled high like a fort,
Inside here, it's a sweet old sport.
The crackling fire's a gentle friend,
As I settle in, my worries mend.

While winters chill wraps all around,
I'm here, the warmth is truly found.
So let the frost be all it may,
I'll stay inside, let's play all day!

Bundled Thoughts of Warmth

Thoughts of spring feel far away,
But let's enjoy this frosty play.
Wrapped in layers like a burrito,
I'm living life like a salty veto.

With each hot sip, the laughter spills,
Against the chill, my spirit thrills.
Crazy socks and goofy hats,
Snuggled tight with all the cats.

The world may freeze, but here I bounce,
In my cocoon, I can announce:
I'm not going out, no way, no how,
Just let me be a couch-bound cow!

Through frosted glass, I'll watch the scene,
As icy blooms curve in between.
I'm stuck in bliss, a winter's dream,
And hibernation's my new theme!

Winter's Whispered Retreat

Snowflakes dance like silly fools,
While I snuggle with my warmest tools.
Outside, the world is crisp and cold,
But here I have my blanket fold.

Sipping cocoa, I laugh with glee,
Chasing away the chill with tea.
The wind may howl, but I won't budge,
I'll stay inside and refuse to judge.

Winter, dear, you cozy old friend,
I promise to meet you at spring's end.
For now, let's play this little game,
Where warmth and laughter rule—no shame.

So raise your cup, let worries cease,
In this season of silence, find peace.
With guffaws and giggles, I retire,
To this fortress of warmth, I proudly aspire.

Cocooned in Silence

Deep inside my fluffy cocoon,
I dream of summer's bright afternoon.
Chirping birds and vibrant skies,
But for now, it's naps and snacks that rise.

Wrapped like a burrito, snug and tight,
I dodge the snowflakes with sheer delight.
Who's that outside? Oh, let them freeze!
I'll snooze away with nap-time ease.

Each tick of the clock makes me smile,
I could stay curled up here for a while.
With no errands, no plans to keep,
This state of bliss, oh, how sweet the sleep.

Let it snow, let it blow, all around,
In my cozy nest, I cannot be found.
While others trudge through rivers of white,
I relish my peaceful, soft twilight.

The Art of Sleeping In

Alarm clocks don't mean a thing to me,
For my bed is where I'm meant to be.
As dawn paints the world in soft hues,
    I just roll over, hug my snooze.

With pillows piled on every side,
The outside world, I will gladly hide.
They say the early bird gets the worm,
    But I prefer my sleepy charm!

You can keep your coffee runs and chats,
    I'll linger here with my cozy cats.
Wrapped in dreams, I float away,
    Who needs a schedule anyway?

So laugh all you want, call me lazy,
In this land of dreams, things get hazy.
Count me in for that glorious sin—
Right here, right now, let the snoozing begin!

Beneath the Blanket of Frost

Beneath a blanket, fluffy and thick,
I lounge like a king, feeling quite slick.
Frost paints the windows like a crazy art,
But here in my kingdom, I'll not depart.

The world outside is sparkling bright,
Yet all I crave is hot cocoa delight.
Who needs adventures? Who needs a chill?
I'd rather stay warm and indulge my will.

Bundled up snug, Netflix on play,
The snow can keep falling; I'm here to stay.
Each chilly gust feels like a tease,
But I'm cozy here, doing as I please.

So here's to the fun of crisp winter air,
While I huddle in warmth without a care.
With laughter and chuckles, let's have a blast,
In the frosty cocoon, this joy is unsurpassed.

The Art of Winter Rest

When the world turns white and cold,
The blankets call, that's what we're told.
Hot cocoa sips and sleepy yawns,
Time to snuggle till the dawns.

Beneath the covers, dreams take flight,
Avoiding chores, with sheer delight.
Who needs gym when couch is near?
An Olympic sport, this cozy cheer!

Icicles hang like frozen swords,
Chasing us indoors, flipping boards.
Winter's chill may nip and bite,
But I'm tucked in; I'll be alright!

So here's to naps and lazy days,
In the fluff of pillows, we'll laze.
As snowflakes dance and windmills spin,
The art of rest? Oh yes, we win!

Embracing Stillness

The world outside is white and bright,
But I'm cozied up, feeling just right.
Silent nights and peaceful days,
In comfy hibernation ways.

Where are my socks? Oh, what a mess!
Under the cushions, I must confess.
They ran away to warmer lands,
Leaving me with iced, cold hands.

Drifting dreams of springtime sun,
But for now, oh, I'll just shun.
A wild raccoon just peeked my door,
Wanna join? I've snacks galore!

Snuggling deeper, don't make a sound,
This festive fluff is my battleground.
So cheers to winter, soft and sweet,
In a comatose bliss, we retreat!

Woodland Dreams in White

The woodland whispers to take a break,
While shadows dance and branches shake.
Wrapped in a cocoon of soft, warm fluff,
Outside it looks quite chilly and tough.

Bears may roam and foxes play,
But here I'll binge-watch all day.
From the window, I'll see them prance,
While munching treats—oh, what a chance!

Sipping tea while the snowflakes fall,
Cuddle up, it's a frosty ball.
Woodland critters, come join my spree,
Napping buddies, just you and me!

Encased in warmth, I'll lay my claim,
To this winter life, it's such a game.
When springtime comes, I'll stretch and shout,
But for now, cozy, there's no doubt!

Frost-kissed Retreats

The frost comes creeping, can you hear?
Whispers of cozy, never fear!
I've set my fort with pillows high,
Let the winter storms start to fly!

Stacked high with snacks and funny shows,
My sanctuary, nobody knows.
With slippers on, I dodge the chill,
Letting warm fantasies distill.

Snowflakes twirl as I take a seat,
Life outside, a circus repeat.
The frost-kissed branches tap my pane,
But here in warmth, I'll stay insane!

So raise a toast to frosted pines,
As I indulge in cheesy lines.
In this little nest, I'll cook and feast,
Until the springtime calls me, least!

The Cozy Den's Lullaby

In a den so snug, I snuggle tight,
Counting dreams like stars at night.
The world outside is cold and gray,
I'll skip the chores and snooze away.

Bears and bunnies join the heap,
While napping soundly, we gently creep.
We'll trade the hustle for a cozy brew,
And nap through ice and cloudy blue.

Fluffy blankets piled up high,
With marshmallow clouds that float on by.
In our lair, the world's on pause,
Who needs the frost? We'll set our cause!

So bring me snacks and peaceful dreams,
With honeyed tea and whipped cream streams.
Yes, winter's chill we'll gladly take,
From cozy nook, let others quake.

Finding Warmth in Wool

Knitted caps and homespun socks,
In my fortress of woolly blocks.
Laying low with cocoa in hand,
I'll trade the world for this soft land.

Sheep are laughing, what a sight,
As I twirl with yarn in the pale moonlight.
"More layers!" they cheer, "Let's bundle tight!"
Tangled thoughts in a woolly flight.

A sheepdog's snooze, a feline's purr,
As heated blankets begin to stir.
We'll hibernate—oh, what a spree!
Who knew wool could be so free?

A toast to fluff and cozy dreams,
In this warm retreat, life's not as it seems.
So, let the snowflakes fall and twirl,
We'll knit our way through every swirl.

Whims of Winter's Whisper

The wind outside, it starts to howl,
I'm snug as a bug, hear me growl.
With cookies fresh and stories grand,
Who needs adventure when I've got sand?

Frosty paws dance on the glass,
While I dream of summer's pass.
But wait! That frozen, chilly bite,
Feels good when wrapped in warm delight.

Snowflakes swirl and twirl about,
While I'm cozy—I've got no doubt.
I'll sip my tea and watch them play,
In my snug retreat, I'll stay all day.

A snowman peeks through frosted glass,
But all I want? For this to last.
Let winter's whim be light and mild,
In my funny nook, forever wild.

A Journey into Peaceful Shadows

In mounds of pillows, dreams enfold,
As winter whispers stories old.
I'll wander through this cozy space,
In shadows soft, I find my place.

Candles flicker with a friendly glow,
While chilly winds silently blow.
With fuzzy socks on, I make a dash,
For snacks that blend with twilight's bash.

Pajamas skilled in weaving cheer,
Make every cuddle full of leer.
As the world lies wrapped in its sleep,
I'll keep my laughter, fresh and deep.

So here I curl, in playful ease,
With secrets shared among the breeze.
Winter's chill, I cheekily borrow,
For in my dreams, there's naught but sorrow!

The Dreamscape of Dusk

As daylight fades, the couch calls me,
My blanket wrapped, a snug decree.
The snacks await, a feast divine,
In this cozy cave, I sip on wine.

The cat is perched, with eyes so wide,
He's plotting naps, oh what a ride!
With every yawn, the world feels slow,
In dreams of cheese, we gently flow.

Time drips like honey, as visions swirl,
The warmth envelops, a soft, sweet furl.
The clock ticks softly, who even cares?
We're kings and queens of comfy lairs!

So let the snow dance, let winter sing,
We hunker down, it's the cozy thing.
When spring arrives, we'll have a chat,
But for now, naptime—how about that?

Reciting Starlit Serenity

The stars twinkle as I curl in tight,
A pillow fortress, oh what a sight!
With popcorn dreams and giggles at play,
Let me snooze my worries away.

The moonlight's glow is a gentle tease,
As silent whispers ride the breeze.
The world can wait, it's way too cold,
I'll crack a smile, or so I'm told.

For in this night, the dreams unfold,
I'm an ice cream giant, bold and old.
With every chuckle, I drift so deep,
Oblivious to promises I can't keep.

So here's to nights that blend and bond,
In our coziness, we grow so fond.
While winter snores and wishes us luck,
Let's hibernate, or just… cluck!

A Winter's Tale of Rest

Snowflakes sprinkle on a sleepy street,
While I nestle in socks, oh what a treat!
With steaming mugs and slippers so grand,
In our lazy den, we make a stand.

The dog's a burrito, snug on the rug,
Dreaming of chasing his favorite bug.
With laughter echoing through this dome,
Winter's stone still, we've made it home.

Candles flicker, the TV hums low,
With each silly movie, our spirits glow.
Wrapped in warmth, the world fades fast,
We'll snooze through the winter, our die is cast.

So here's to rest, let it gleefully swell,
In this cozy cocoon, all is well.
For when bright blooms return, we'll be ready,
But for now, dear winter, let's keep it steady!

The Calm Before the Thaw

The frost blankets rooftops, white and bright,
As I snuggle closer, snug and tight.
With comic books piled high as the sky,
Adventures await, oh my, oh my!

The chilly air prompts a playful cheer,
A chorus of snorts, and lots of beer.
We take on the world, using just our beds,
The best kind of war is fought in our heads!

While squirrels scurry, oblivious and spry,
We're the couch potatoes, oh my, oh my!
With dreams of summer, but winter's our jam,
Here in this bubble, we give a grand slam.

So raise up a mug to the snowy delight,
We'll dance with the blankets all through the night.
For soon enough, the thaw will be here,
But until then, let's keep winter near!

Napping Through the Blizzards

Snowflakes fall, the world is white,
Time to snuggle, oh what a sight.
Pajamas on, with cocoa in hand,
Blanket forts in winter's land.

Socks in hand, I wiggle my toes,
Against the chill, my sleepy nose.
The fridge is stocked with snacks to munch,
I'll snooze away without a hunch.

Outside there's frost, but I don't care,
A comfy couch is my throne of flair.
Chilly winds, go blow and roar,
I'll just nap, who could want more?

Midday dreams, they drift and soar,
While I'm snugged up behind the door.
Winter's wild? A comical jest!
I choose the fluff of a cozy nest.

A Quiet Retreat from the Chill

The wind howls like a howling beast,
While I prepare my napping feast.
Hot tea brews, with cookies near,
A world of warmth, let's disappear!

Frosty windows, a chilly pane,
But here inside, there's joy, not pain.
A blanket fort? Oh, what a dream!
In my soft cocoon, life's a gleam.

The fireplace crackles, I feel the heat,
While snowflakes tumble in a snowy feat.
Let them dance, let them swirl around,
I'm in my paradise, safe and sound.

The world can wait, it's time to play,
In cozy nooks, I'll choose to stay.
No icy paths, no frosty calls,
Just laughter, warmth, and cozy walls.

Hibernal Nightfall

Daylight fades, the sun sinks low,
Wrap me tight, let the games slow.
Candles lit, a shadowy dance,
In winter's grip, I take a chance.

The blankets pile, a fluffy mound,
While snowstorms rage without, profound.
I crack a smile, no real worries,
As squirrels prepare their little flurries.

The clock ticks by—a gentle pace,
Fuzzy socks replace the race.
Outside, the shivers do their part,
But in here, I'm cozy at heart.

So let the dark of night enfold,
With cookies, cocoa, tales retold.
In hibernal glee, I'll choose my themes,
A night of laughter, and warmth, and dreams.

Beneath the Blanket of Silence

Whispers of snow in the quiet night,
I pull my covers, oh what delight.
Soft pillows beckon, oh so sweet,
A lazy life, the winter's treat.

Chills outside might dance and play,
But here I settle, dream the day away.
Furry creatures, all tucked in tight,
While I chuckle at the frosty bite.

With snacks all set and stories near,
Every sip of cocoa warms the cheer.
In this embrace, I hold the key,
To winter's nap and fuzzy glee.

A stillness wraps, a cozy cloak,
As outside the blizzards twist and poke.
In dreams, I roam on warmest tides,
While winter's laughter fades and hides.

Sheltered in Serenity

Under fluffy blankets we snugly lay,
Ignoring the world, come what may.
With snacks on our laps, and shows to binge,
We giggle and laugh, while winds do cringe.

Our beds are our castles, oh, what a sight,
King and queen of the couch, it's pure delight.
With hot cocoa in hand, cheers to the freeze,
Who needs to step out? We do what we please!

The snowflakes may dance, the chill may bite,
But inside we're cozy, wrapped up tight.
The outside may storm, but we won't flinch,
We'll nap through the chaos, not even a pinch.

So let it snow, let the cold winds blow,
We're hibernating with snacks in tow.
With a sigh of content and a wink of the eye,
We'll stay burrowed here, just you and I.

Cradled by the Cold

The frosty winds howl, but we're blissfully warm,
In our pajamas, we brave every storm.
With a pile of soft pillows and cozy delight,
We cherish this time as the world gets white.

Outside there's a snowman with a carrot nose,
But all that we see are our toes and woes.
With laughter and snacks, we're a jolly old crew,
Who needs the sun? We've got plenty to do!

Hot tea in one hand, a cookie in the other,
We're huddled together, oh, sister and brother.
The world can keep spinning, we'll take our own pace,
While the cold does its worst, we'll just stay in this place.

The fireplace crackles, we giggle and cheer,
In our winter wonderland, there's nothing to fear.
Wrapped up in laughter, we all take a chance,
To enjoy the stillness, and just do the dance!

In the Heart of the Winter Nest

In our winter nest, it's snug as a bug,
With blankets and laughter, we give a big hug.
The fluffy pillows pile high to the sky,
Here we'll stay comfy, oh me, oh my!

The trees may be bare and the ground all white,
But inside our cave, it feels just right.
Hot cider is brewing, oh the scents that delight,
We raise up our mugs, saying cheers with a bite!

While outside the critters scurry and flee,
We're in our own bubble, just you and me.
The flakes keep on falling, but we won't budge,
Why would we venture? We just love our grudge!

So we'll nap and we'll snack while the cold winds wail,
We're snug as can be — it's our happy tale.
With giggles that echo, we're cozy and bright,
In the heart of our nest, everything feels right!

Shadows in Sleigh Bells

The snowflakes outside put on quite a show,
While we're tucked in tight, moving ever so slow.
The sleigh bells ring out, but we let them be,
Wrapped up in fun, just your friend and me.

With marshmallows floating in our mugs of cheer,
We're charmingly lazy, in our cozy sphere.
Outside it's a blizzard, but inside we glow,
With popcorn and giggles, we're ready to flow.

The world can be frosty, it won't get our vibe,
We're a team of delight, with snacks and our tribe.
Let the cold winds blow, let the snowflakes fall,
In the warmth of our laughter, we shall have it all!

So ring out the jingle, let the joy unfurl,
With shadows and giggles, we dance and twirl.
In our fortress of warmth, we laugh through the night,
As the winter wraps 'round, we're cuddled up tight!

Fluid Frost and Peaceful Paws

The chilly winds blow through the trees,
As critters cozy up with perfect ease.
All the squirrels have tucked in their tails,
While rabbits dream of soft, warm trails.

The frosty air brings giggles and cheer,
As they snuggle up close, no worry or fear.
With blankets of snow all fluffy and bright,
Each furry friend knows it's time for the night.

In this frosted realm, they dance and they play,
Avoiding the cold, oh what a grand ballet!
They frolic and scamper, their laughter like bells,
As they chase snowy dreams, where warmth always dwells.

So let's raise a toast to the snug little bunch,
With cookies and cocoa, it's time for a munch!
Here's to padding paws and the warmth of the sun,
In the land of the sleepy, all worries are done.

Glimmers of a Softened Heart

When days grow short and shadows play,
The world slows down in its cozy way.
The trees wear blankets, the sky wears gray,
But we find joy in this sweet ballet.

The kittens curl up, all purring with glee,
Imagining summers so bright and free.
They dream of the fields where they can run wild,
While snuggling close, like a child's soft smile.

Though nature dozes, we're not really blue,
For laughter and joy are in our zoo.
With hot cups in hand, we sit by the fire,
With stories and jest, our hearts all aspire.

So raise up your mugs, friends, here's to the freeze,
To warmth in our homes, and a chill in the breeze!
Though the world may be cold, our hearts shine so bright,

With fun in our souls, we'll dance through the night.

The Quiet of Fallow Fields

In fields so still where the snowflakes drift,
The rabbit's nose twitches, seeking a gift.
Beneath all the chill lies a world full of fun,
Resting till spring brings the warmth of the sun.

The branches all yawn, the berries take heed,
Creatures are napping, fulfilling their need.
As the world quietly wraps in its white,
We gather our cheer, with twinkles of light.

Frost-dusted leaves make a carpet of dreams,
While critters plot mischief, or so it seems.
In laughter we tread, on this chilly terrain,
With giggles and wiggles, we'll dance in the rain.

So here's to the moments of peace and delight,
In fields wrapped in silence, all cozy and bright.
May our hearts find their joy like snowflakes that land,
In the sweet, soft embrace of this wintery land.

Untangling in the Thaw

As frost melts away, we stretch and awake,
With laughter and light, make no mistake!
Those snuggly routines begin to dissolve,
In warmth and in sunshine, our troubles resolve.

The playful pups pounce, like they own the place,
While squirrels dance round with their zippy race.
They tumble and twirl, in a frolicking spin,
As the world shakes off its dull, winter skin.

With each radiant beam, all spirits get high,
As crocus and daffodils reach for the sky.
We sip on our drinks with a hearty ol' cheer,
The balm of warm breezes is finally here!

So let's dance in the sun, shake off winter's gray,
Break free from those layers, in our lively play!
With joy in our hearts, we can prance without care,
For the thaw is our stage, and we're all welcome there.

Moments Suspended in Time

The world outside is frosty white,
While I snuggle up, it feels just right.
Blankets piled high, I'm snug as a bug,
Time slows down, like a cozy hug.

Hot cocoa in hand, I sip with glee,
The wind howls loud, but not near me.
Shadows dance by the fire's warm glow,
What a sight—so much fun, don't you know?

The fridge is stocked, I'm not going out,
List of snacks? Oh, it's a long route.
Wooly socks on my feet, I wiggle and squirm,
This lazy life? It's my favorite term.

So let the snowflakes fall on the street,
My fortress of blankets cannot be beat.
In my cozy den, I'll joyfully play,
Moments suspended in time—hooray!

Whimsy in Winter's Embrace

Winter's here, the trees wear white hats,
Where's my sled? Oh, look at the cats!
They chase shadows and pounce on snow,
But me? I've got hot tea in tow.

A snowman awaits, all lopsided and grand,
His carrot nose—oh, how poorly planned!
With arms of twigs, he gives me a nod,
"Stay inside," he says, "that's not so odd!"

I toss on my coat, venture outside,
But cheeky flakes make me want to hide.
I slip and I slide, oh what a sight,
Then retreat to my hearth, feeling just right.

In my snug fortress, I stifle a laugh,
Watching the world while I sip my craft.
Whimsy in winter's embrace, can't you see?
Let the snowflakes swirl; they can't capture me!

Savoring the Silence

The silence of winter, oh, what a treat,
No sounds but my tummy's occasional tweet.
It's the season to munch and nibble away,
Savoring the silence of each lazy day.

Outside, the kids play, all bundled and bright,
While I sip on my soup, oh, what pure delight!
The quiet wraps snugly, like a big, fluffy coat,
Instead of the hustle, I find joy in a moat.

With each passing hour, the soft shadows creep,
What a nice reason to nap and to sleep!
With a book on my lap and a sigh that just flows,
I'm savoring silence—forget all my woes.

Winter whispers sweetly, like a lover's tune,
In this soft, snowy cocoon, I swoon.
So let the world bustle, I'm happy to rest,
Savoring the silence, now that's my quest!

Flickers of Quietude

In the still of the night, with a flickering light,
I snuggle up tight, feeling cozy and bright.
The world outside sparkles, all fresh and new,
But inside my lair, it's just me and my stew.

Flickers of quietude fill the room,
As I munch on some cookies, avoiding the gloom.
The clock ticks softly, it won't miss a beat,
While I wave to the snowflakes from my comfy seat.

The neighbors are out building forts in the snow,
But I've got my book; oh, where did the time go?
With each crushing crunch of a snack that I munch,
The world feels so tasty, all calm in a bunch.

So here I will be, toasty warmth all around,
Laughing at flakes as they tumble to ground.
Flickers of quietude dance in the air,
In this snug winter bubble, there's nothing to spare!

Chronicles of the Cold

When the frosty winds start to blow,
I ponder my fate, should I stay or go?
The couch calls my name, cozy and bright,
Why face the blizzard when I can take flight?

Cupcakes are safe, buried deep in the stash,
While snowflakes outside make a splendid splash.
With blankets piled high, I'm ready to nap,
Who needs the outdoors? I'm snug in my trap.

The world can freeze over, I just don't care,
With cookies and tea, life's a soft chair.
The birds may be chirping, doing their thing,
But I'll stay right here like a lazy spring.

So gather your mittens, I'll wave goodbye,
From under my mountain of flannel, oh my!
The chronicles of cold are just beginning,
As I dream of sunshine while winter's still spinning.

Sweet Repose in Ice

As frost paints the windows, I tuck in tight,
Fluffy pillows and snacks make everything right.
The north wind's a-whistling, it's not that scary,
I'll just hunker down with some chocolates to carry.

With Netflix to binge, and no calls to make,
Who needs the outside? Just one little break!
The world can be frozen, I hold the remote,
While others are shivering, I'm busy to gloat.

Socks on my feet, coffee steaming with glee,
I'm sweetly secluded—now that's my decree!
While icebergs march forth like a snowy parade,
I'll snooze right here, never feeling betrayed.

So let winter storm rage and icework take sway,
I won't be unwrapped 'til the sun comes to play.
With marshmallows floating like dreams in my cup,
Sweet repose in ice, it's just too good to pass up!

Sheltered from the Whirlwind

The trees are a-shiver, the sky's a fierce gray,
Yet here I am snuggled, all cozy and gay.
The blustery world can rage and can howl,
While I munch on popcorn and give winter a scowl.

Each flake that falls is a tickle to tease,
But I'm wrapped like a burrito, so bring it, please!
With marshmallow fluff and some cookies made round,
Life's a sweetest shelter and joy can be found.

The ice may be thick and the roads may be slick,
But I'm grounded right here, it's a real winter trick.
While snowflakes spin wild, round and round like a twirl,

I'll toast to my blanket; it's soft and it's pearl.

So howl all you want, I won't have a care,
With snacks piled beside me, no need for fresh air.
Sheltered from the whirlwind, I'll take my sweet stand,
In this light-hearted don't-care winter wonderland!

In the Depths of Winter's Pause

As the frost creeps in on the windows with style,
I throw on my pajamas, and settle for a while.
The wind may be howling, but I'm not awake,
In the depths of winter, it's my time to bake.

With hot cocoa brewing, the vanilla is grand,
While out in the fray, they shovel the sand.
But all I can think, as I snuggle up tight,
Is how best to nap through the long, chilly night.

The world can be snowy, the skies gray and wide,
But I'll stick to my sofa with cuddles inside.
A playful reminder of warmth's gentle glow,
My blankets are fierce warriors, quiet and slow.

So cheers to the winter and all that it brings,
Muffled giggles amidst all the flings.
In the depths of winter's pause, oh what a treat,
To cozy and chuckle, right here, with my feet!

The Call of the Cozy Cave

The sun is bright, but I'm still in my bed,
Chasing dreams inside my fluffy head.
With snacks piled high and blankets so wide,
I'll wait for spring from my cozy side.

Outside the snowflakes spin and sway,
But here in my cave, I wish they'd stay.
I'll build a fortress made of fluff,
And laugh at winter's icy cuff.

The fridge is stocked, the hot cocoa brews,
Why venture out when I've got these views?
I hear the winter calling my name,
But the couch is winning this lazy game.

So here I lie, just a little more,
In this snug retreat, I could not ask for more.
When the world is cold, my fire's aglow,
I'll let the neighbors brave the snow.

Dreaming Beneath Frosted Canopies

The trees stand tall with a frosty gown,
While I dig deeper, won't come down.
Tucked away in my flannel wear,
I could nap forever, so warm and bare.

Outside a snowman shivers and shakes,
But I'm buzzing dreams with holiday flakes.
Why face the chill when I can cuddle?
Your icy sidewalks just burst my bubble!

The world can freeze, the winds can howl,
But in my lair, there's no need to scowl.
With cookie crumbs and cozy socks,
I'll laugh at winter as I rest in blocks.

Under layers thick, I drift away,
In this cloud of warmth where I'll remain.
The snow can fall, and the wind can wail,
I'll stay inside, my warmest tale.

Cocoon of Cold

Into a cocoon, I gracefully fold,
Wrapped in blankets, no worries, no bold.
The world outside can freeze and fight,
While I binge-watch shows in soft, dim light.

The air is nippy, like biting ice,
But my fortress of fluff feels oh-so-nice.
Why venture out with the frost's tight grip?
A comfy world is my favorite trip!

Sipping hot tea and nibbling some pie,
Through the window, I watch the flakes fly.
Wild squirrels dance and then they hop,
But I'm in my warm stew, I'll never stop!

When spring arrives, we'll have a ball,
But till then, it's cuddles and not much at all.
For now, I thrive in this cocoon of bliss,
Where winter's chill turns into warm kiss.

Whispers of the Winter Den

In my winter den, the snacks abound,
As whispers of cold swirl all around.
With fuzzy socks and a hat, I grin,
Here's to my couch, oh let the fun begin!

The outside world can freeze and shiver,
While inside, I dance—oh, what a quiver!
With dance moves like a sleepy bear,
I'll whirl and twirl without a care.

Mugs of cocoa like treasures displayed,
While the snow makes shadows that slowly fade.
I'll toss snowballs from my magical nook,
If only I could, more snacks to cook!

So here I'll stay, in my joyful den,
As the snowflakes fall, again and again.
With laughter and snores, what a merry scene,
Who knew winter could feel so serene?